a long rainy season

contemporary japanese women's poetry, volume 1

THE ROCK SPRING COLLECTION OF JAPANESE LITERATURE

a long

HAIKU & TANKA

rainy season

edited and translated by
leza lowitz, miyuki aoyama, and akemi tomioka

with illustrations by robert kushner

The editor wishes to gratefully acknowledge the generous support
of the National Endowment for the Humanities.

Acknowledgment is also made to the editors of the following publications
in which some of these translations first appeared:
Winds, Tokyo Journal, Harper's, Noctiluca, Yellow Silk, Shearsman, Tokyo Today, and *ZYZZYVA.*

Published by STONE BRIDGE PRESS
P.O. Box 8208 • Berkeley, California 94707
TEL 510-524-8732 • FAX 510-524-8711

Cover and interior illustrations by Robert Kushner.

First on-demand edition, 2002.

10 9 8 7 6 5 4 3 2

Printed in the United States of America.

Library of Congress Cataloging-in-Publication Data

*A long rainy season: haiku & tanka / edited and translated by Leza Lowitz, Miyuki Aoyama,
and Akemi Tomioka; with illustrations by Robert Kushner.*
      p.   cm.——(Contemporary Japanese women's poetry; vol. 1)
      "The Rock Spring collection of Japanese literature."
      ISBN 1-880656-15-9.
      *1. Japanese poetry——women authors——Translations into English. 2. Japanese
poetry—— 20th century——Translations into English. 3. Haiku——Translations into
English. 4. Waka——Translations into English.   I. Lowitz, Leza.   II. Aoyama, Miyuki.
III. Tomioka, Akemi.   IV. Kushner, Robert.   V. Series.
PL782.E3L66   1994
895.6'1040805——dc20   94-28749
                                                        CIP*

dedicated to

hamasaburō aoyama

(1923–1993)

contents

HAIKU

TANKA

Note to readers about Japanese names: Names of writers and other Japanese people referred to in this book appear in Western order—family name last—except for premodern literary and historical figures, who appear family name first and are customarily known by their given or "art" names. Macrons ("long signs") are used to aid pronunciation of Japanese names except for those names of writers whose published work in English regularly appears without them.

introduction

It has been said that Japanese women writers, unlike their counterparts in the West, have never had to create "a room of their own" because there was always an accepted place for them in the literary world. This place, however, was the realm of the imperial court, where women were indispensable to the creation of Japan's earliest extant collections of poetry, the *Manyōshū* (Anthology of Ten Thousand Leaves, ca. A.D. 780) and the *Kokinshū* (Collection of Ancient and Modern Times, ca. 905). A third of the poems in the *Manyōshū* are by women, and twenty-eight women writers are represented in the *Kokinshū*, the first of twenty-one imperial anthologies. The three poets who contributed the most poems to the fourth imperial anthology, the *Go-Shūishū* (Later Collection of Gleanings, ca. 1086), which contained 1,218 poems, were women—Lady Izumi contributed 67; Sagami, 40; and Akazoe'emon, 32. Also, of the 2,211 poems in the seventeenth imperial anthology, the *Fūgashū* (Collection of Elegance, compiled 1344–49), a woman, the empress Eifukumonin, composed 69. And of course it was a woman of the court, Lady Murasaki, who wrote *The Tale of Genji*, the eleventh-century masterpiece considered the first great novel in world literature. While their male contemporaries were also versifying in the "high culture" language of imported Chinese, the women writers of the Japanese court were mostly perfecting expression in their native language. Their poetic legacy of elegance and technical skill had a lasting impact on the country's aesthetic.

Today's Japan, however, is vastly different from courtly Japan a thousand years ago, and so are its women writers.

Japanese women's literature has always been closely tied to the cultural and social context in which it was created. In the Heian period (A.D. 794–1185), the time of Lady Murasaki, women court poets wrote sensual and achingly beautiful *waka* ("Japanese verse"), later called *tanka* ("short verse"). An experience was not considered complete until a waka—only thirty-one syllables long—had been composed to mark the occasion. Furthermore, one's desirability as a lover was often determined by the quality of one's verse. At the same time, these passionate verses often included subtle forms of social criticism or wry commentary on male-female relationships.

Over the next six hundred years—a very long stretch of time—itinerant women storytellers spread the oral tradition through shamanistic folk tales, Shinto legends, verse, music, and dance. During the Meiji period (1868–1912), when Japan's modernization began full force, the Japanese government promoted the "good wife, wise mother" role that stressed the virtues of raising a family and caring for in-laws, thus affording women few opportunities to write or publish. One of those women who did publish, however, reflected a new boldness in her art. It was Akiko Yosano, whose 1901 collection, *Midaregami* (Tangled Hair), revitalized the ancient form, mentioning the word "breasts" for the very first time in confident and explicitly sensual tanka. By the early Taishō period (1912–26), Japan had undergone immense social change in the process of westernization, and women had begun to fight for educational, legal, and social rights. Women writers began to openly embrace these new freedoms in poems and essays, particularly those published in Japan's first feminist literary magazine, Raichō Hiratsuka's *Seitō* (Blue Stocking). The poetry magazine *Myōjō* (Morning Star), published by Akiko Yosano's husband, Tekkan, was a major influence on Japan's new Romantic poets, while women's popular magazines such as *Fujin Kōron* (Women's Forum, 1918) and *Nyonin Geijutsu* (Women's Arts, 1928) supported women's growing consciousness. A political group for women, the Shinfujin Kyōkai (New Women's Association), was established in 1919 by Fusae Ichikawa and Mumeo Oku, whose political savvy and strength inspired many women to fight for equality and political power.

Haiku, on the other hand, was traditionally the realm of male poets in Japan, as poetry in Chinese (called *kanshi*) had been in Heian times. This simple seventeen-syllable form had evolved from the poetic sequences used to create *renga,* or "linked verse," and was originally called *hokku* or *haikai.* Created in rebellion against the decorum of formal waka and renga composition, haiku emerged in the sixteenth century. Matsuo Bashō (1644–94), a former samurai, perfected the form, creating humorous and moving poetry from ordinary objects and experiences. Haiku took on increasing importance as a bridge between the experiential world of the poet and the world of natural phenomena. Independent of the aristocratic social values that had surrounded the composition of waka, Bashō wrote that haiku was essentially useless and alluded to how it probably could not be understood by most people—"a brazier in summer and a fan in wintertime."

After Bashō's death the form continued to thrive and be reinvigorated by Yosa Buson (1716–84), Kobayashi Issa (1763–1827), and Masaoka Shiki (1867–1902), who wrote and taught haiku. This tradition continues today, as haiku poets study in poetry societies under the tutelage of famous *sensei* and publish journals reflecting their groups' particular styles and concerns. One such early journal was Shiki's Meiji-period magazine *Hototogisu* (Little Cuckoo). With its poetry group of the same name, it was considered the dominant voice in haiku for decades.

Following the Great Kantō Earthquake that leveled Tokyo in 1923 and throughout the militaristic 1930s until World War II, the burgeoning feminist movement of the Taishō period was suppressed, and the Meiji-period virtues of modesty and selflessness—serving first one's parents, then one's husband, then one's children—once again prevailed. After the war—which had a devastating impact on the populace, both in terms of the human toll and the psychological repercussions of defeat—women were expected to devote themselves to providing stable family environments for children, hard-working husbands, and aging in-laws, this time in the effort to help rebuild the country after the war.

During the American Occupation and into the 1960s, free verse poetry emerged as a strong cultural force, having been influenced over the years by the Romantic poets, French symbolism, jazz, the Beat Generation, and other movements. Women free verse poets formed a strong literary community, often as a result of having been marginalized. Dozens of literary magazines were established at that time, including those for women such as Sachiko Yoshihara and Kazue Shinkawa's influential feminist magazine *La Mer*, with its regular readings in the Tokyo atelier.

The early 1960s brought antiwar protests to college campuses, while the mid-1970s saw the birth of Japan's feminist movement, many of whose members came from the student movement. Inspired by the publication of Erica Jong's *Fear of Flying* and *Ms.* magazine, Japanese women lawyers, writers, and activists formed the "Pink Helmet" Group and later the Women's Action Group. Two magazines for women, *More* and *Croissant*, also began at this time and are still popular today, although, like *Ms.*, they have altered their image to keep up with the times.

The 1980s were a period of unprecedented industrial vigor, but seeds of discontent were evidenced by violence within Japanese high schools. With the Japanese economy finally stable, many Japanese women were able to turn to the community, supporting school functions and engaging in social activities with their children. As citizens sensed the end of an era, the desire for social change became more visible during Emperor Hirohito's illness until his death in 1989. By the boom years of the late 1980s to the early 1990s, young Japanese women were showing less interest in traditional family-centered lifestyles and more interest in traveling abroad, enjoying material pleasures, and pursuing careers. Although women now make up forty percent of the Japanese workforce and over half of the employees in large companies, they are mostly confined to dead-end secretarial jobs as "OLs," or "office ladies." Even female graduates of Japan's best universities find it hard to advance; they say their education often only helps them find a similarly well-schooled husband, should they choose to do so.

Still, the late 1980s saw many gains for women, among them the election of the first woman to high political office (Takako Doi of the Japan Socialist Party became Japan's first woman

Speaker of the House of Representatives in 1993). The past five years have brought other women into new positions of power, such as Japan's first female Supreme Court justice. The ministers of the Economic Planning Agency, the Environmental Agency, and the Ministry of Education are women, and Japan recently appointed its first female train conductor (who has a master's degree from the prestigious Tokyo University) and its first woman astronaut. Granted, these gains may not seem momentous when compared to those of Western countries, but they do represent significant achievements in a country that is notoriously slow to change.

How is this social climate reflected in contemporary women's haiku and tanka? It is generally thought that Japanese women are twenty years behind their Western counterparts. However, if that were the case, Japanese feminism would be in its heyday now. It is not. Feminism, like any other movement, takes many individual forms. It is also culturally defined. Therefore, some Western readers might feel that these poems concern limited, mostly domestic themes. This is partly due to the limited realm of activities that Japanese society affords its women members and to the lingering Confucian-based emphasis on motherhood as the realm most appropriate for women. It is also due to the subtle nature of these short forms of Japanese poetry.

In the act of writing, Japanese women have had to rebel against those deeply ingrained Confucianist values and, in some cases, to completely reject them. Although most of the three generations of women poets in this anthology lead normal lives within accepted standards—many are married, have children, and write when they can—some have chosen to leave their husbands and families or to remain single and work to support their writing. It should be noted that when social criticism has been present in Japanese poetry, it has generally not been revealed directly, but through suggestion. In that sense, the advantage of the short forms is that they both magnify and distill moments that might otherwise be missed—moments in the everyday lives of women, for example.

Although I have outlined the social background of women in Japan in brief and broad strokes, it is my belief that the poems in this volume should be looked at from the inside out rather than from the outside in, as they speak eloquently for themselves.

HAIKU AND TANKA

The seventeen-syllable haiku, traditionally made up of three syllabic units of five, seven, and five syllables, is the shortest form of poetry in the world—a haiku takes less than five seconds to recite. Historically the haiku traces its lineage back to the first part of a waka, the highly formalized Heian-period court song arranged in a sequence of 5-7-5-7-7 syllables. The waka form evolved into renga (linked verse), which became popular in the Kamakura period (1185–1333). Renga were written in a kind of call-and-response poetic dialogue in which a three-syllabic-unit 5-7-5 verse was composed by one person, followed by a two-syllabic-unit verse of 7-7 syllables composed by another person in response. This was then followed by another 5-7-5 verse, and so on, until the linked verses sometimes became over a hundred lines long. The first three syllabic units of the renga gradually took on a semi-independent function as the *hokku* ("beginning verse"); considered the most important, memorable verses, they set the tone for what followed.

Masaoka Shiki used the hokku as an independent form (as the poet Matsuo Bashō had done before him), giving it the name "haiku" in the late nineteenth century. From then on, these words were no longer considered solely the beginning phrases of a long linked verse. As a self-contained short poem, the haiku was used to distill the universe through the juxtaposition of dissimilar elements while creating unity through the use of a seasonal word (*kigo*). As seasons are tied to the life cycle, seasonal references give the poem vitality and rhythm. Also a part of the evolved haiku aesthetic are strains of Shinto animism and the Zen Buddhist conviction that anything can offer the opportunity to achieve enlightenment. The haiku poet, although working with commonplace imagery and experience, can nevertheless evoke profound feelings and sensibilities.

Contemporary Japan has thousands of amateur poets, and many experts in other professions write poetry as a hobby, such as Nobel Prize–winning scientists and department-store scions. The number of writers of haiku alone is estimated to be between five and ten million. According to Makoto Ōoka, a poet and former president of PEN Japan, a few thousand professional haiku poets write, teach, appear on TV or radio, publish magazines, and earn a reasonable living through these efforts. In fact, Japan may be the only country in the world where poets can actually make a living writing poetry.

Despite haiku's more down-to-earth origins, many modern and contemporary women poets have found the strict rules of haiku composition stifling and the hierarchical atmosphere of haiku contests intimidating. Always closely linked to the natural world, a haiku—according to most, but not all, theorists—had to employ seasonal words, contain a strict syllable count per line, and preferably include literary allusions to poems past. Some poets, however, including Hōsai Ozaki (1885-1926), departed from seasonal words and other conventions quite successfully. Still, mastering any one of these techniques takes years of practice. Japanese society, after all, considers that haiku poets do not begin to develop their true talents until age 65, and the average age of famous haiku poets today is over 50. Of the postwar women writers who studied and practiced the form, many were eventually awarded high positions in official haiku organizations, a development that reflects both their talent as poets and the gains women writers have made in the traditionally male-centered world of Japanese haiku. Symbolic of those gains, in 1955 the important haiku magazine *Hototogisu* was taken over by the poet Teiko Inahata after the death of her father, who had inherited the magazine from *his* father, the poet Kyoshi Takahama.

Stylistically, contemporary women haiku poets generally retain a connection to formal traditions. Continuing the tradition of self-portrayal that began with Bashō, the poet Nobuko Katsura makes the "I" a female who is completely objectified and wholly identified with nature. In the haiku from which the title of this book is taken, for example, the images of breasts and rain create a startling juxtaposition that radiates acceptance and wisdom. Breasts bear down upon the woman in the same way the rain bears down on the land during the rainy season. Underlying this is the fact that both sustain and nurture the country. (Breasts feed children and rain fuels rice crops.) Yet the long rainy season, with its unrelenting downpour, inevitably ends and summer begins. Katsura's poem depicting wanderers against the background of the red moon echoes the tradition of writing haiku during long and arduous travel. Several of the haiku poets here refer to the naming of things, perhaps a reference to the fact that naming places is left to those in power, while singing of those famous places was historically the realm of waka poets. Haiku poets traditionally take as their subjects the unsung scenery, the small valleys and fields they encounter in their wanderings.

The use of seasonal words is particularly skillful in Teiko Inahata's haiku, which include references to New Year's, a period considered a fifth season for haiku purposes and a time of great renewal in Japanese culture. Inahata's awareness of light and shadow, sound and silence reflects a heightened spatial sense and acceptance of universal opposing forces. Keiko Itō uses seasonal words to reveal in her modern style a slightly anachronistic "old Japan" of *tatami* mats, bamboo flutes, and the shrine at Ise dedicated to the sun goddess. Kiyoko Uda's haiku takes as its seasonal words animals such as fireflies (summer), dragonflies (autumn), crabs, horses, and flying fish, while Sonoko Nakamura's humorous image of her father shaking out leaves from a tree is in keeping with the wit and lightness of the haiku tradition. Kōko Katō's magnification of the universe in fine brushwork, such as eyebrows, reflects the Zen spirit.

For 1,200 years, tanka has been the most popular form of verse in Japan. Ninety percent of the poems in the *Manyōshū* are tanka, as are 991 of the 1,111 poems in the *Kokinshū*. Formerly called waka, or "Japanese song" (to distinguish them from poems written in Chinese), poems in this form consist of five syllabic units containing thirty-one syllables in the pattern of 5-7-5-7-7. (The first three 5-7-5 lines split off early on and evolved into the haiku.) Formal devices such as the stylized fixed epithets called "pillow words" (*makura-kotoba*) and the double-meaning "pivot words" (*kake-kotoba*) are rarely used by contemporary women tanka writers, who tend to find them old-fashioned or cumbersome to employ.

Modern tanka saw its first major reform with the movement begun by the poet Naobumi Ochiai (1861–1903), who encouraged younger poets such as Akiko Yosano to explore more overt passions in the ancient forms. Takuboku Ishikawa (1886–1912), a member of the group centered on the magazine *Myōjō*, attempted to radicalize tanka, but his naturalistic style and shift in form ultimately failed to take root in tanka and instead catalyzed the free verse movement. Mokichi Saitō (1882–1953) was able to forge an artistic compromise. Women tanka poets continue to revitalize the age-old poetic form by enlarging the tanka realm beyond poems of heartache and passion to embrace a larger world. In a country where something "new" can still be two hundred years old, this is an achievement not to be overlooked.

Fumi Saitō's tanka reflect the tremendous creative adventuring of the 1960s in a philosophical exploration of the dualities of reality and art, the universe of God and the created world of the poet. Saitō's tanka exhibit a painter's sensibility that uses traditional seasonal images as artful anchors in occasionally surrealistic poems. Winter becomes a "frozen nerve," horses are drawn out of a canvas, black gloves become anthropomorphized flowers, the face of an *ukiyo-e* painting by Sharaku comes alive, and the museum—typically a place of unchanging art—is transformed into an element of nature with incredible momentum.

Meiko Matsudaira's tanka offer a different kind of artistry: a sensual nostalgia is conveyed in decorative language that pays homage to the woman of the Heian court while revealing the decidedly independent persona of the modern thirty-something single woman. The appeal of Marxism and the heady ideals of the student movement prior to the breakdown of the leftist party is reflected in the elegaic and politically conscious tanka of Motoko Michiura, who uses traditional seasonal imagery like flowers against the background of tear-gas clouds and lonely jail cells. Emphasis on the family as a social unit and on the woman as the head of that unit can be seen in the work of Yūko Kawano, who explores the life cycle and, in other works, evokes an awareness of race and history and the self-consciousness of the writer and her place in the world.

The life of the single, working woman of the 1990s is epitomized in the colloquial tanka of the two young poets Machi Tawara and Amari Hayashi. Tawara uses conventional seasonal words like fireworks and tulips but combines them with "borrowed" foreign words, product names, overt abstractions, and philosophical reflections, such as direct comments on loneliness and freedom. Her poems often use a highly unusual split narrative perspective to convey emotion. Amari Hayashi takes a more direct and light approach to sexuality and the body; her refreshing frankness and cynicism reflect changing attitudes toward the body. Her use of graphic images and, along with Motoko Michiura, the mention of menstruation in her tanka break long-standing taboos.

Taking this aspect one step further is Ei Akitsu, whose poems reflect a quirky humor and down-to-earth bawdiness not often found in the decorous tanka. Her tanka explores the untapped universe of a woman's body, perhaps even making the female form into a new kind of poetic "season," rich in unexplored possibilities. With hanging ovaries and bamboo groves within the body, traditional Japanese seasonal references are inverted and dissected. Akitsu's tanka doesn't just give us the supple autumn persimmon, but takes us inside the persimmon tree, whose forces are literally bursting. "If you give birth," she says, "give birth to the world." The poet and her universe are reflected in the magnified "down and dirty" images of a dog's testicles and the smell of shit on a hand. She also makes jabs at Japan's traditional symbol of transient beauty, the cherry blossom, which to her is "unpleasant." Thus, when Akitsu writes about her ovaries in a tanka, purists might be shocked, just as they might have been when Bashō wrote about his horse pissing by his pillow one sleepless night on his travels. Still, what Bashō did three hundred years ago was revolutionary, and many of the writers in this anthology are writing poems that are individual acts of rebellion today.

ABOUT THE TRANSLATION

The American poet, critic, and translator Kenneth Rexroth compared the 1960s and early 1970s flowering of Japanese women writers to the Heian court period, but not since Rexroth and Ikuko Atsumi's *The Burning Heart: Women Poets of Japan* (1977) has there been a substantial collection of Japanese women's poetry available in English. That was almost twenty years ago, and most of the women in that anthology were from ancient times. Recent anthologies of contemporary Japanese poetry, such as *From the Country of Eight Islands* (1981), *A Play of Mirrors* (1990), and *The New Poetry of Japan* (1993), have included the work of only a few women poets. Yet the mainstream success of recent books of Japanese poetry translated into English—*The Ink Dark Moon* containing poems of the Japanese women court poets Ono no Komachi and Izumi Shikibu (1988, translated by Jane Hirshfield and Mariko Aratani), and *Salad Anniversary*, Machi Tawara's well-received first collection of tanka (1989, translated by Juliet Winters Carpenter)—indicated a growing interest in Japanese poetry abroad.

As a student of poetry and later a lecturer in creative writing with an interest in Japanese literature, I read widely in ancient Japanese poetry and sometimes taught it to my students. While there was much to be learned from the styles and concerns of the women writers of the Heian court, my students—many of whom were poets, and most of whom were women—wondered, as I did, what Japanese women poets today were writing. It was this curiosity that led me to seek out the work of Japanese women poets in the hopes of introducing them to my students. To my surprise, I found little to nothing available in translation. This motivated me to search out the works on my own and to attempt to create an anthology. When I came to Tokyo in 1990 and began to collaborate with Miyuki Aoyama on the project, I knew the process of locating poets through introductions, word of mouth, or discovery in literary journals and poetry groups would be challenging, to say the least.

Once we had found the poets, we asked them to submit poems they felt best represented, in style and content, their concerns and talent. We then selected poems with regard to excellence in craft and technique, originality and vision. Theme and content were considered separately, as well as in light of the other works selected. In the end, we made our selection according to taste. Did we love the poems? Did they have to be included? If the answer was yes, we chose to include them.

The original objective of this anthology was to introduce the most important living women poets of Japan to Western readers. But what, after all, does "important" mean? In the process of soliciting manuscripts, we discovered that many important poets had written their best works twenty or more years before, or had stopped writing poetry entirely. Younger poets, as well, had reservations about whether their work was good enough to be included with older, more established writers. Likewise, some of the more established writers refused to be in the book because they did not want to be grouped together with younger, and in their estimation, inferior talents.

As a woman who wrote poetry and was influenced by the women poets of ancient Japan, I wanted to read contemporary Japanese women's poetry and through it, to discover what kinds of lives women were living in Japan today. My intention in compiling this anthology was to introduce the work of poets I was moved by to Western readers in English. As with any selection, the one represented in this book is not definitive. Undoubtedly there are poets who have been left out. In order to represent the current situation in Japanese women's poetry today, we have included both renowned and unknown poets here; only three of them have been recently translated into English.

The poems were translated through collaboration and extensive rewriting. Two of the editors are poets themselves, so a non-literal approach was taken to capture the spirit of the original verse as we saw it. In both the haiku and tanka, the English was not put into a strict syllable count, since we felt this would force the works into the straitjacket of rhythm rather than allowing the inherent rhythms of the language to emerge. In many cases, particularly in the tanka, the poets themselves did not strictly adhere to syllable count.

We have translated the haiku in a three-line format and the tanka in a five-line format, with the exception (at her request) of the tanka of Amari Hayashi, who writes tanka in two lines rather than a single line and who wanted to retain that format in English. The difficulties of translating Japanese are often commented on, such as the lack of articles to indicate singular or plural. As an example of our style and concerns, we include the following version of a tanka by Machi Tawara. The original Japanese reads:

> *Chūrippu no/ hana saku yō na/ akarusa de/ anata watashi o/ ratchi seyo nigatsu.*

When directly translated this becomes

> tulip flower/ bloom like/ brightness/you me/ carry away February

which we rendered as

> You,
> bright as a tulip in bloom—
> take me
> away
> in February.

Another version (in a translation by Juliet Winters Carpenter) doesn't use specific pronouns, drops a preposition, and refers to more than one flower, but is equally effective:

> With the gaiety of tulips in bloom
> carry me off—
> February.

All our selections and translations necessarily reflect our interpretation of the individual works and our literary taste. We often took creative license, particularly at the expense of literalness. All responsibility for the translations, of course, is ours.

Professor Makoto Ueda of Stanford University termed translation a form of literary criticism as well as artistic creation, but it was Baudelaire who said that poets are the "universal translators" because they translate the language of the universe—stars, water, trees—into the language of humanity. It is our hope, then, that this book enriches and expands the universe of those who read it and paves the way for more collections of its kind in the future.

ACKNOWLEDGMENTS

This book started as a dream, and the fact that it has become reality at all is largely due to the support, goodwill, and hard work of many people. Namely, I would like to thank David Korr of the New York University School of Dramatic Writing for introducing me to the cinemagraphic aspects of ancient Japanese poetry and Robert Hass of the University of California at Berkeley for teaching me the lyrical aspects. Kathleen Fraser of San Francisco State University provided the impetus for this book and led me to Momoko Watanabe, whose eagerness to help led me in turn to Miyuki Aoyama, without whom this book would surely still be a distant dream and to whom I am deeply indebted. Akemi Tomioka weathered some storms to produce excellent translations, and Junko Abe was always there for me in good humor when I asked about *kanji*. Many others offered valuable insights, home-cooked meals, hot sake, and equally nurturing words of wisdom during late nights of work, especially Shogo Oketani, Helen Taschian-Tappan, Eric Gower, Kyoko Michishita, Maryann Fleming, Abigail Davidson, Richard Ruben, Kazuko Shiraishi, Geraldine Harcourt, Bonnie Nadell, La Loca, Elizabeth Wood, Sherry Reniker, George Evans, Cid Corman, Jane Hirshfield, Yuri Kageyama, Stephen Shaw, Tom Chapman, Ed and Chako Ifshin, Edgar Honetschläger, Peter McMillan, Hiroaki Sato, and Donald Richie. *Taihen kansha shite orimasu* to Eric Feldman and the Feldmans, who brought me to

Japan and offered encouragement every step of the way; to my indefatigable agent, Tatemi Sakai of Orion; to Robert Kushner, for the original artwork he created for this book; and to my publisher, Peter Goodman, whose patience with midnight faxes and belief in this project spurred me on. I would like to especially thank John and Fran Lowitz, Donna and Dave Mendelsohn, who wondered if I would ever come "home" again, the Sugiuras, Hamasaburō Aoyama, and Tazuko Aoyama, who took care of Miyuki's children while she worked on the translations and taught a full courseload. Thanks as well to Tōru Arai, who offered valuable insights and suggestions on translation, and to Kiichirō Tomioka for his patience, understanding, and love. Finally, all of us who worked on this anthology would like to express the utmost gratitude to the poets themselves, for writing these poems, sometimes despite considerable odds.

Leza Lowitz
Tokyo, Japan
Summer 1994

HAIKU

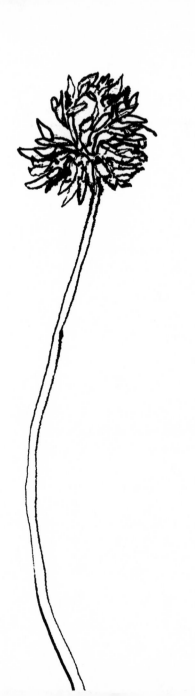

nobuko katsura

*is currently vice president of the Modern Haiku Association of Japan
and the editor-in-chief of the literary magazine SŌEN (Garden of Grass).
She was born in Osaka in 1914 and began writing haiku under the
direction of the poet Sōjō Hino. Later she became a founding member of
the haiku group Marumero (Quince) with Kenkichi Kusumoto. Her
book FRESH GREEN (1974) received the Modern Haiku Award for
Women. Her other major works are MOONLIGHT (1949)
and WOMAN'S BODY (1950).*

Someone else's wife—
green garden peas steamed gently
in hot water.

The nuisance
of breasts—
a long rainy season.

Outside the window, snow;
a woman in a hot bath,
water overflowing.

My mother's soul
viewing the plum blossoms,
returning at night.

A stalk of bamboo—
someone in white
passing by.

End to end, side to side—
Mount Fuji spreading into
the summer field.

Under the cloudy sky
I walk deep into the mountains—
blossom season.

In a withered winter forest
running, not getting lost,
a man on horseback.

A cicada, singing at dusk
falls from a pine tree,
still dripping.

A crow in the rainy season
cries,
"Shūson is dying, dying."*

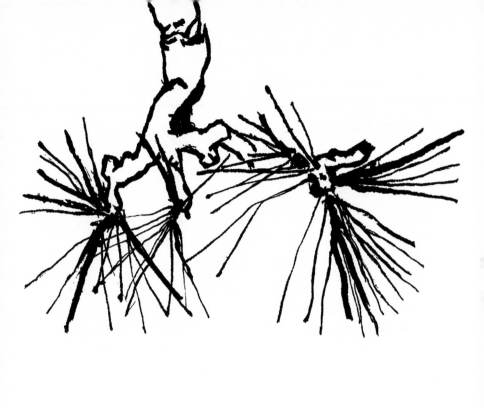

A snake
hiding in a hole in a tree—
shining black.

Wearing white—
absolutely no way out of it
these days.

kimiko itami

was born in 1925 and received the 19th Modern Haiku Association Award for her book MEXICAN SHELL. She has written eight books of haiku, including TIME TRAVELING and AUTUMN IN PERTH, four volumes of poetry, and a volume of travel sketches. She is interested in an existence which embraces all human beings and rises above the concerns of the individual.

Weaving thoughts
of cotton—
summer solstice woman.

What lives in the lake
filled with a blue
that has no name?

I got a Mexican shell
from a boy with the eyes
of a pirate.

Can eternity
stay on my palm? A garden
of Chinese quince.

Fish with an ancient
face, caught
in a winter river.

Twilight at a port of call—
smell of daffodils
and steel.

The wedding reception in progress:
a fake view
of the Pacific Ocean.

For my mother,
dying,
the clear Himalayan star.

Chickweeds holding out their
    supple hands—
the steel-framed construction
is coming along.

Rain
on the eucalyptus tree
like infinite thought.

sonoko nakamura

was born in Shizuoka Prefecture in 1913 and attended Nihon Women's University, but left school before graduation. She has written numerous books of haiku and has received many awards, including the Modern Haiku Association Award. Currently over 80 years old, she is still teaching haiku at five different schools in Tokyo.

My father
up in the treetop, shaking out
spring leaves.

A bell always rings
at dusk
in the water.

Land-locked bride
tempted offshore—
the open sea.

Under the sea
there might be a city,
I wash a peach.

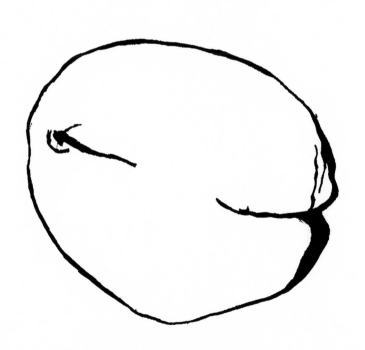

Red moon—
one wanderer, two wanderers
disappear in the valley.

A married woman:
in the distance
a spring trumpet blows.

teiko inahata

has been writing haiku since her childhood. Her grandfather was the
master haiku poet Kyoshi Takahama, and her father was the famous poet
Toshio Takahama. She is currently haiku editor for the ASAHI SHINBUN,
the largest daily newspaper in Japan. She has edited the literary magazine
HOTOTOGISU (Little Cuckoo) since her father's death. Inahata has
written many volumes of poetry, essays, and criticism, including THE
HAIKU OF TEIKO (1976), THE HAIKU OF TEIKO II, (1985),
and THE LIGHT OF SPRING (1986). Born in Yokohama in 1931, she
received her education at Kobayashi Seishin Women's College.

First calligraphy of the year—
too much force
in my brushstroke.

The first laugh
of a baby's life,
made without sound.

Young leaves of iris;
a refreshing wind
comes and goes.

A deep canyon,
the moon behind it—
where did it come from?

With the look
of chasing a butterfly,
I join.

Against the *shoji* screen—
the muse's
shadow.

kiyoko uda

was born in 1935 and is an instructor of haiku at the NHK Culture Center in Osaka. She has written three volumes of haiku, titled LILAC TREE, SUMMER DAYS, and PENINSULA. She has received the Modern Haiku Association Award.

In the tedium
of the evening prayer,
crabs emerge.

Window in the
pleasure quarters!
Glint of flying fish.

May, come quick!
the earth at the horse's hooves
has fallen in.

Dead fireflies—
the night skies have cleared
beautifully.

Half-alive
dragonfly, drying
against a stone.

Soul and breasts
in my arms
in autumn.

Pond smelts:
both the living and the dead
arch their bodies in the air.

For a waterlily
and a man and a woman—
the afternoon is long.

How long!
the falling of a bolt of lightning
from beginning to end.

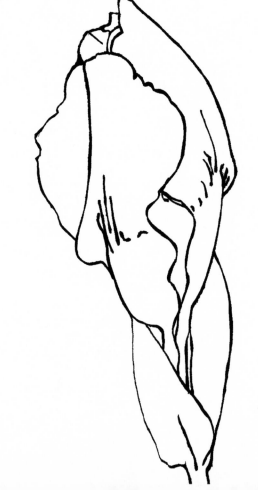

Having strayed from his son,
the father in a summer hat
begins to walk.

Irises—
plucking a single stalk
I go to see him.

All the butterflies in the field
I hide
in my breast.

Wheat—
with such certainty
we assume death completely yellow.

kōko katō

was born in 1931 and is president of the Kō Poetry Association, secretary
of the Japan Haiku Association, and councilor of the International Haiku
Exchange Association (to name a few of the organizations she belongs to).
She is publisher of KŌ, a bilingual (Japanese and English) poetry journal
that is dedicated to peace and mutual understanding. She has published
many volumes of haiku, including PICTURES OF OWARI, and books of
criticism, including HAIKU IN ENGLISH, DAYS, and FOUR SEASONS,
a bilingual book about seasonal themes in haiku.

An eyebrow raised
slightly;
sound of bird.

Chagall's women—
clouds of springtime
arriving.

Vast field of flowers;
the sail of a cloud passing
slowly.

Onto a hundred silver trees
the moon drops
blue dew.

Muffled in white breath—
voice of the
heart.

Michinoku*—
a thousand ricefields growing green
where he once walked.

keiko itō

was born in 1935 and is editor-in-chief of the haiku magazine SASA
(Bamboo Grass). She has published seven volumes of haiku as well as
many volumes of essays and criticism. Her main works are
A BUNDLE OF NIGHT and NARUMI VARIEGATION.

Two wild daffodils
growing together—
separate scents in the air.

A hazy moon—
the sea constantly rages
in Ise.*

Like striking an axe,
a bamboo flute is sounded—
first festival of the year.

In each mind
fireworks glow
from afar.

Pleasant voices
in a room—
summer tatami mats.

Like the sound of a fire crackling;
river snow,
melting.

TANKA

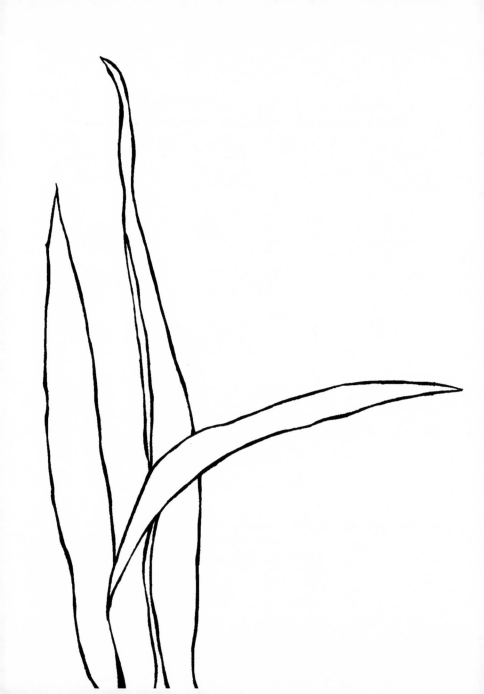

ei akitsu

was born in Fukuoka Prefecture in 1950. She has published many books of innovative tanka, including TO LILY MAGNOLIA, OPIUM, and FAINT WHITE LIGHT, all to critical acclaim. Her SELECTED POEMS has just been published. She is particularly interested in the position of women writers in modern Japanese society, and has been at the forefront of efforts to organize symposiums, lectures, and readings with other women tanka poets.

Ah, women
walking with ovaries
hanging inside—
the wind blows, the bamboo groves
cry from within.

Crepe myrtle!
Isn't there a man
who will give himself
up to me
to be ruined?

Sorting out
the groundless sorrows
of the afternoon
with disposable
chopsticks.

"Why was I given breasts?"
I wonder,
coming to town
to buy toothpicks
in the cold afternoon.

Now,
well into the afternoon:
how strange
to smell shit
in the palm of my right hand.

I leave my house
preoccupied with thoughts;
a dog with saggy balls
passes
on the street.

Asphalt pavement
being torn up:
there goes another
homo sapiens
with swollen breasts.

Being a perfect George Sand
I leave the shop
face refreshed,
a Japanese radish
in my arms.

Resisting the need
to pee,
I walk through a belt-like park
covered with
fallen bush clovers.

Even though we've kissed—
even though we've spoken—
you are you
I am
me.

Inside the Japanese persimmon tree
forces erupt
vermillion,
bearing fruit
over the treetops.

If you give birth
give birth to the world—
buds bursting
in the fresh green
woods.

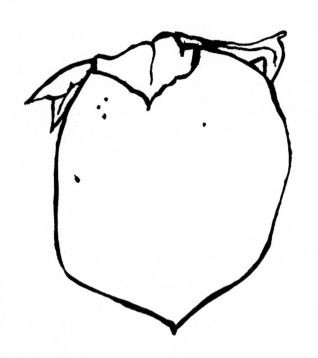

Dissecting
the Virgin Mary's abdomen—
dim purple womb
one summer
evening.

Sharp sickle
of heaven—
off with my head!
Since I'm living my life
like a giant slug.

This morning's sadness
passed away
as I wiped the sweat
off my nose
again and again.

A ball of flesh
bobbing in a swing,
a lead weight hanging
from the sky—
this we call a child?

After my bath
I dry
my steaming breasts
as if wiping
my soul.

I wish
every word
I spin
into my work
were glorious opium.

Unpleasant—
the cherry blossoms
slowly swelling
from yesterday
to today.

motoko michiura

was born in Wakayama Prefecture in 1947 and graduated from the literature department at Waseda University in 1972. She received the 25th Modern Tanka Society Prize for the 1980 publication of HELPLESS LYRICISM. She has published four books of poetry, including A DAY LILY and WOMEN'S AND MEN'S TANKA. She is also the author of an illustrated book of tanka called TANKA AT THE WATER'S EDGE (1991). She is well known for her poetry concerning her experiences as a student activist at Waseda in the 1960s and 1970s. She is currently an instructor of poetry at the Asahi Culture Center.

Washing and combing
the smell of tear gas
from my black hair—
I go out
to see him.

Suddenly,
rising from my breast
hidden to protect me
from tear gas:
the smell of lemon.

Dead of night
returning home exhausted
from the interrogation—
my period begins to flow
like rage.

Up on the roof
I'll stand until
I become the flag,
knowing
tomorrow will come.

If you love him
love him
to destruction;
a yellow day lily
bending to the wind.

Bud of youth
in a prison cell—
all day long
thinking
of you.

It's September;
released
from
wifehood
I stand on wet green grass.

From the lips
that sing
no lullaby
blows a spring wind
of sorrow.

Ah, my pocketbook
slipping off my shoulder
to my waist—
not even feminism
can save me!

Someday
I'll turn to water—
that's when
the blood of my parents
will come to an end.

Water marries, grasses marry, trees marry
and wind marries
but man marries
making woman
gloomy.*

Okinawan girl
tearing down the
flag of the Rising Sun;*
I want to hold her
in my arms.

Walking through the streets
in my torn stockings—
where does
this misery
come from?

Father,
becoming single once more,
I suffer from
having been born
a woman.

Breasts that know nothing
of nurturing a child
when I wrap them
in Turfan silk
they turn young again, and new.

The country where the emperor lives
and countries where emperors
no longer reign—
could there be a difference
between them?

Lightning
pierces the sky—
gunfire
in a pacifist country
this autumn evening.

One of those men
in his forties, worn out,
Mr. Marxist's sleeping face
looks like
a blade of grass.

My nipples
still erect,
I fall into a sleep
that won't dive into
making love.

meiko matsudaira

is best known for her tanka depicting the life of a thirty-something divorcee living on her own in the city. Born in Aichi Prefecture in 1954, she joined the Cosmos tanka group in 1976 and graduated from Nanzan University with a degree in Japanese literature the following year. In 1977 she was awarded the 23rd Kadokawa Tanka Prize. Her books of tanka include LIKE MY FATHER UNFURLING A SAIL (1979), BLUE NIGHT (1983), SUGAR (1989), PLATINUM BLUES (1989), and A DREAM NARCISSUS (1991), a collection of selected tanka. She was awarded the first annual Aiko Kawano Tanka Award in 1991.

Light crimson bush clovers
scattered and gone;
love is like gilt
coming off
after all.

Warm wine
from his mouth
to mine,
lapping against me
radiating through me.

Arms, glistening
in the water as they swim,
clutch the pool's edge
needing no
interpretation.

Light snow,
falling like down.
White salt,*
covering
everything.

The days of my twenties
come back to me
with a glint of
heat-haze weariness!
Scratches on enamel.

Sweet osmanthus
burning its incense
day by day,
scattering embers
of small golden flowers.

On an autumn day
when anything transparent
looks forlorn,
many a stemmed glass
begins to sing.

The bubbling
of rosé champagne—
the sound
of stars
coming and going.

Happiness
is
like the
tinge of green
in white wine.

Here, the cherry blossoms
are throwing away
their platinum lives;
evening twilight
deepens.

Passion unspoken
congeals,
growing into a black pearl
deep
in my body.

yūko kawano

was born in 1946. She is the award-winning author of many volumes of tanka as well as essays and critical works. Her main works are LIKE A WOOD, LIKE A BEAST, CHERRY BLOSSOM FOREST, and BINDWEED. She is the tanka editor for the MAINICHI SHINBUN, one of the largest daily newspapers in Japan.

Giving birth or being born—
either the ultimate sorrow.
Just the same,
I turn the light out
at night.

When I
(womb for an unborn child)
sink into sleep,
rain sets in to the darkness
like some primeval ocean.

Climbing the mountain pass
our two children
between us:
this is
a family.

A child,
having drawn a great ellipse
on a white paper,
steps into it and
plays by himself.

My son waits for me
just across the way.
I will probably age
with this distance
between us.

Wretched
are my two children
blown along with me
a mast in a gust—
day after day.

Among a school
of swimming children
I see my children's
black hair—
that's the Asian race.[*]

Powerless in Japanese,
his mother tongue,
my eldest child comes home today
defeated again
by English.

I am Japanese
I am Japanese—
knowing this,
I won't let myself or my poetry
be lessened.

I am
the woods and
the beast:
the sea-blue sky
sharpens my hearing.

Carry me off
as if scooping up
fallen leaves
in one stroke,
won't you?

You, approaching me
with the smell
of freshly cut
morning grass—
my nipples turn hard.

fumi saitō

was born in Tokyo in 1909, and has been the editor-in-chief of the literary magazine GENKEI (Prototype) for over thirty years. She has written numerous volumes of tanka and essays. Her most famous works are FISH SONGS (1940), THE DIRECTION OF A SONG, and CRIMSON (1976). She is the winner of the Choku Award in poetry (1977) and the Yomiuri Award in literature (1986), among others. She is the daughter of the writer Ryū Saitō.

On my frozen nerve
there is a place
where a red canary
comes
to perch.

Horses—
hearing the sound of the wind
I draw them
out of the canvas
and make them take off.

Black gloves
I threw into a field
rise up again—
yellow flowers blooming
from their fingers.

Shamisen music floating down—
a mouth painted black
by Sharaku*—
an unexpected smile
from the corner.

I emerge
from the museum
at dusk—
the blue Nile
floods over.

Wearing the hazy heat
I flicker and sway
like a spirit:
a dog
is startled.

Snow plays more lightly
in the empty sky
than me—
stalling
and falling.

What melts
with the snow
in the springlike afternoon?
A pearl
loses its gloss.

Lit up
from the side of death,
life may not
always be
shining and crimson.

It could be a bird
fluttering over
the mountain pass—
it seems young,
its voice light green.

The sight of a bridge
without people or horses
crossing it—
just a bridge
spanning out.

chieko yamanaka

has written eleven volumes of tanka, as well as many books
of criticism and essays. Her main works are SPACE
LATTICE (1957), SPINDLE, and STARS.

Behind Mount Miwa*
the mysterious moon rises—
I wonder who first
gave it
a name?

Watching the cherry blossoms shimmer,
break through the sunshine;
I was born to be human
in this dark,
transient world.

The droning of cicadas
fades behind me
like a stone weight—
I've got your letter
with me.

Leo at springtime
lifting his feet
in the midnight sky—
you,
the eternal traveler.

Skylark in February
chirping in this filthy world—
we always call things "God"
if they
cannot be explained.

amari hayashi

was born in Tokyo in 1963. In addition to publishing several books of
poetry, among them MARS ANGELS, THE SECOND-TO-LAST-KISS,
and SHORT CUT, she has written two books of essays, including THE
END OF THE CENTURY IS A MADEMOISELLE. She also writes
criticism about alternative theater and has written a theater guide,
entitled THEATERS: THESE MYSTERIOUS FRIENDS. She was
baptized a Christian in 1978. She writes her tanka deliberately
in two lines, a distinctive format reflected here in the way the
English translation has been set in type.

You could pluck the cosmos
    if you slept with a hundred men:
a girl laughs
    in the fields.

Woman comes to a bed
    without refusing—
scents of tea from many countries
    on her pillow.

"That girl? She left
    here yesterday," one says.
"No, she hasn't
    come yet," says another.

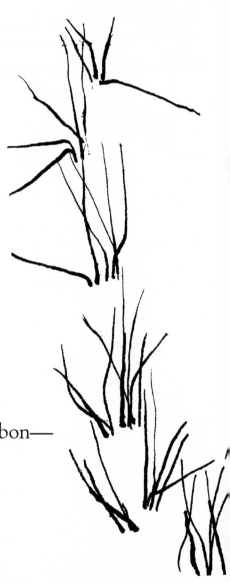

Gently tying
    and untying a ribbon—
why could I tie it
    so well before?

Her head is moving:
   is it nodding yes or shaking no?
Yes, no one
   will ever really know.

At daybreak
   I wake up crying—
intimations of rain
   and future heartaches.

The sound of static
    as he quickly pulls his tie off—
the man's neck
    begins to shine.

Fucking hotly
        during my period—
the two of us stare earnestly
        at the pool of blood.

Hunting for the place
    where body odor is strongest—
"Go for the woman
    who smells the most!"

Having done
      the most insincere thing,
how can you look at me
      with such clear eyes?

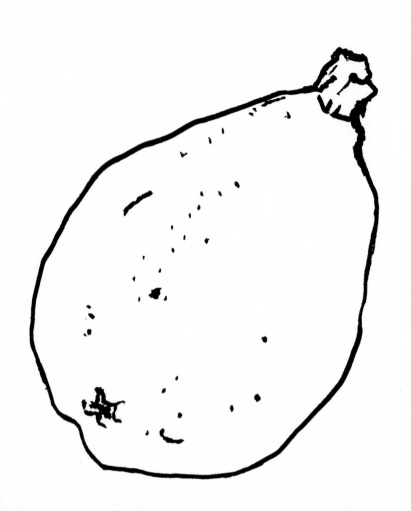

Dark stairs
    in a strange city—
I feel more lonely
    with your hand down my pants.

I finger the
     lace on my collar
until night, when you
     turn over my petals.

machi tawara

was born in Osaka in 1963 and graduated from the literature depart-
ment of Waseda University in 1985. She is the author of the ground-
breaking collection of tanka, SALAD ANNIVERSARY, which sold over three
million copies and became one of Japan's all-time bestsellers—in any
genre. "August Morning," the book's opening fifty-poem sequence, received
the prestigious Kadokawa Tanka Prize, and SALAD ANNIVERSARY was
selected the outstanding poetry collection of 1987 by the Association of
Modern Poets. Tawara's other books include FRESHLY PICKED TANKA,
FOUR-LEAFED ESSAYS, BECOMING WIND, THE TEARS
OF AN APPLE, and PALM OF THE WIND.

Changing trains
as if folding up
an umbrella—
I return
to my hometown.

Fireworks, fireworks
watching them together—
one sees only the flash
the other,
the darkness.

Loving each other
and being together
mean different things to each of us
sudden rain,
sunny day.

Getting by
giving each other
room to grow;
sometimes
freedom can be lonely.

This flying
we call falling—
petals smile
unexpectedly
revealing naked sprays.

Like the word "if"
the lives we once led
are
a
void.

Palm of the
wind—
fanning
specks of light
across the Shimanto River.

Staring out at the horizon
each of us
lost in thought—
a lighthouse flashing
on and off.

You,
bright as a tulip in bloom—
take me
away
in February.

notes

Translations of all haiku, some tanka by Motoko Michiura, and all tanka by Fumi Saitō, Chieko Yamanaka, Amari Hayashi, and Machi Tawara are by Leza Lowitz and Miyuki Aoyama. All other translations are by Leza Lowitz and Akemi Tomioka.

The following text notes are referenced by page number:

38 Shūson Katō was editor-in-chief of the important literary magazine *Kanrei* (Cold Thunder) and one of the most influential haiku poets in modern Japan. He died on July 3, 1993, at the age of 88.

68 Michinoku is the ancient name for Mutsu province, which comprises present-day Fukushima, Miyagi, Iwate, and Aomori prefectures. It is frequently mentioned in haiku. The poet here is referring to the haiku Bashō wrote when he traveled there.

70   Ise refers to the eastern districts of Mie Prefecture and the location of the ancient shrine to the Shinto sun goddess.

110   The *kanji* for marriage (*kon*) is a combination of the characters for "woman" and "gloom."

111   Okinawa, off southern Japan, was the site of the fiercest battles of the Pacific War, in which 150,000 civilians were reportedly killed. Many Okinawans today harbor tremendous animosity toward the imperial system in whose name the war was waged, a symbol of which is the Rising Sun flag.

123   The custom of sprinkling salt in the doorways of Japanese restaurants and traditional-style buildings derives from Shinto purification rituals.

140   The author and her family lived in the United States in 1984.

151   Tōshūsai Sharaku was an enigmatic Edo-period *ukiyo-e* painter about whom very little is known. His extant work was done in 1794–95 using a then-revolutionary mica-dust technique.

162   Mount Miwa is in present-day Nara Prefecture, famous for its cryptomeria, and is frequently written about in haiku and tanka.

bibliography

The following publications were consulted in the preparation of this book.

ANTHOLOGIES OF MODERN AND CONTEMPORARY JAPANESE LITERATURE AND POETRY

Davis, Albert R., ed. *Modern Japanese Poetry*. Translated by James Kirkup. Queensland: University of Queensland Press, 1978.

Fitzsimmons, T., and Yoshimasu Gozo. *The New Poetry of Japan*. Santa Fe: Katydid Books, 1993.

Hibbett, Howard. *Contemporary Japanese Literature*. New York: Alfred E. Knopf, 1977.

Keene, Donald. *Modern Japanese Literature: An Anthology*. New York: Grove Press, 1956.

———. *Dawn to the West: Japanese Literature in the Modern Era*. New York: Holt, Rinehart and Winston, 1984.

Kijima, Hajime. *The Poetry of Postwar Japan*. Iowa City: University of Iowa Press, 1975.

Morton, Leith. *An Anthology of Contemporary Japanese Poetry*. New York and London: Garland Publishing, 1993.

Ninomiya, T., and D. J. Enright. *The Poetry of Living Japan*. London: John Murray, 1957.

Ōoka, Makoto. *A Play of Mirrors: Eight Major Poets of Modern Japan*. Santa Fe: Katydid Books, 1987.

Rexroth, Kenneth, and Ikuko Atsumi. *The Burning Heart: Women Poets of Japan*. New York: Seabury Press, 1977. Reprinted as *Women Poets of Japan*. New York: New Directions, 1982.

Sato, Hiroaki. *Ten Japanese Poets*. Hanover, N.H.: Granite Publications, 1973.

——— and Burton Watson. *From the Country of Eight Islands: An Anthology of Japanese Poetry*. New York: Columbia University Press, 1986.

Shiffert, Edith, and Yuki Sawa. *Anthology of Modern Japanese Poetry*. Tokyo: Charles E. Tuttle, 1972.

Ueda, Makoto. *Modern Japanese Poets and the Nature of Literature*. Stanford: Stanford University Press, 1983.

TANKA AND HAIKU

Beichman, Janine. *Masaoka Shiki*. New York: Twayne, 1982.

Blyth, R. H. *Haiku*. 4 vols. Tokyo: Hokuseido Press, 1949–52.

Brower, R. H., and Earl Miner. *Japanese Court Poetry*. Stanford: Stanford University Press, 1961.

Carpenter, Juliet Winters, trans. "Twenty-five Tanka from Five Women Writers." *Japanese Literature Today* 17 (March 1992). (Published by Japan Pen Club, Tokyo.)

Carter, Steven. *Traditional Japanese Poetry: An Anthology.* Stanford: Stanford University Press, 1991.

Corman, Cid, and Susumu Kamaike, trans. *Back Roads to Far Towns: Bashō's Oku no Hosomichi.* New York: Grossman, 1968.

Cranston, Edwin. *A Waka Anthology.* Stanford: Stanford University Press, 1993.

Giroux, Joan. *The Haiku Form.* Tokyo: Charles E. Tuttle, 1974.

Hamill, Sam, trans. *Narrow Road to the Interior.* Boston: Shambhala, 1991.

———. *Only Companion: Japanese Poems of Love and Longing.* Boston: Shambhala, 1992.

Henderson, Harold G. *An Introduction to Haiku: An Anthology of Poems and Poets from Bashō to Shiki.* Garden City, N.Y.: Doubleday Anchor Books, 1958.

Higgenson, William, and Penny Harter. *The Haiku Handbook.* Tokyo: Kodansha International, 1985.

Hirshfield, Jane, and Mariko Aratani. *The Ink Dark Moon: Love Poems by Ono no Komachi and Izumi Shikibu.* New York: Vintage Books, 1990.

Levy, Ian Hideo, trans. *The Ten Thousand Leaves: A Translation of the Man'yōshu, Japan's Premier Anthology of Classical Poetry.* Princeton: Princeton University Press, 1981.

McCullough, Helen Craig. *Kokin Wakashū: The First Imperial Anthology of Japanese Poetry, with "Tosa Nikki" and "Shinsen Waka."* Stanford: Stanford University Press, 1985.

Miner, Earl. *Japanese Poetic Diaries.* Berkeley: University of California Press, 1969.

Murasaki, Shikibu. *The Tale of Genji*. Translated by Edward Seidensticker. 2 vols. New York: Random House, Vintage Books, 1990.

————. *The Tale of Genji: A Novel in Six Parts, by Lady Murasaki*. Translated by Arthur Waley. New York: Modern Library, 1960.

Nippon Gakujutsu Shinkōkai, ed. [1940]. *The Man'yōshu: One Thousand Poems Selected and Translated from the Japanese*. New York: Columbia University Press, 1968.

Pekarik, Andrew. *The Thirty-Six Immortal Women Poets: A Poetry Album with Illustrations*. New York: George Braziller, 1991.

Rexroth, Kenneth. *One Hundred Poems from the Japanese*. New York: New Directions, 1964.

————. *One Hundred More Poems from the Japanese*. New York: New Directions, 1976.

Sato, Hiroaki. *One Hundred Frogs: From Renga to Haiku to English*. New York: Weatherhill, 1983.

————. *String of Beads: Complete Poems of Princess Shikishi*. Hawaii: University of Hawaii Press, 1993.

Stamm, Jack, trans. *Tawara Machi: Eigo Taiyakuban Sarada Kinenbi* [Machi Tawara: "Salad Anniversary," Bilingual Edition]. Tokyo: Kawade Shobō Shinsha, 1988.

Stryk, Lucien. *On Love and Barley: Haiku of Bashō*. New York: Penguin Books, 1985.

Tawara, Machi. *Salad Anniversary*. Translated by Juliet Winters Carpenter. Tokyo: Kodansha International, 1989.

Ueda, Makoto. *Modern Japanese Haiku: An Anthology*. Tokyo: University of Tokyo Press, 1976.

————. *Bashō and His Interpreters*. Stanford: Stanford University Press. 1991.

Waley, Arthur, trans. *The Uta*. Hawaii: University of Hawaii Press, 1976.

Yosano, Akiko. *Tangled Hair: Selected Tanka from "Midaregami."* Sanford Goldstein and Seishi Shinoda, trans. Tokyo: Charles E. Tuttle, 1987.

ANTHOLOGIES OF CONTEMPORARY JAPANESE WOMEN'S FICTION

Birnbaum, Phyllis, trans. *Rabbits, Crabs, Etc.: Stories by Japanese Women.* Hawaii: University of Hawaii Press, 1982.

Lippit, Noriko, and Kyoko Selden, eds. *Japanese Women Writers: Twentieth Century Short Fiction.* Armonk, N.Y.: M. E. Sharpe, 1991.

Mitsios, Helen, ed. *New Japanese Voices.* Boston: Atlantic Monthly Press, 1992. (Contains several stories by women writers.)

Miyoshi, Masao, ed. *Manoa* 3, no 2 (1991). Featuring contemporary fiction (and some poetry) by Japanese women.

Tanaka, Yukiko, ed. *To Live and To Write: Selections by Japanese Women Writers, 1913–1938.* Seattle: Seal Press, 1987).

—— and Elizabeth Hanson, eds. *This Kind of Woman: 10 Stories by Japanese Women Writers.* Stanford: Stanford University Press, 1982.

OTHER WORKS ABOUT JAPANESE WOMEN

Bernstein, Gail, ed. *Recreating Japanese Women 1600–1945.* Berkeley: University of California Press, 1991.

Iwao, Sumiko. *The Japanese Woman: Traditional Image and Changing Reality.* New York: Free Press, 1993.

Lebra, Takeo. *Japanese Women: Constraint and Fulfillment*. Hawaii: University of Hawaii Press, 1984.

Pharr, Susan. *Political Women in Japan*. Berkeley: University of California Press, 1981.

Sievers, Sharon. *Flowers in Salt: The Beginnings of Feminist Consciousness in Modern Japan*. Stanford: Stanford University Press, 1983.

White, Merry. "Home Truths: Women and Social Change in Japan." *Daedalus* 121 (Fall 1992).

OTHER WORKS OF INTEREST

Drake, Christopher. "On Translating Japanese Poetry and Poetic Prose." *Proceedings of the 1st International Japanese-English Translation Conference.* (Hakone, Japan), 1990.

Fowler, Edward. "Rendering Words, Traversing Cultures: On the Art and Politics of Translating Modern Japanese Fiction," *Journal of Japanese Studies* 18 (Winter 1992).

Keene, Donald. *The Pleasures of Japanese Literature*. New York: Columbia University Press, 1988.

Mamola, Claire. *Japanese Women Writers in English Translation: An Annotated Bibliography*. New York: Garland Publishing, 1991.

Ōoka, Makoto. "Antidote for Anomie: Poetry for the Computer Age." *Japan Foundation Newsletter* (Tokyo), August 1992.

Paz, Octavio. "Translation and the Subversion of Plurality." *Daily Yomiuri* (Tokyo), October 22, 1990.

Sato, Hiroaki. "Modern Women Poets of Japan." Paper presented at the National Arts Club, New York, February 25, 1994.